Beyond Toddlerdom Tips

Quick fixes for keeping five- to twelve-year-olds on the rails

DR CHRISTOPHER GREEN

Vermilion
LONDON

7 9 10 8

First published in Australia and New Zealand in 2004 by
Doubleday

First published in the United Kingdom in 2004 by
Vermilion, an imprint of Ebury Press
Random House UK Ltd.
Random House
20 Vauxhall Bridge Road
London SW1V 2SA

www.randomhouse.co.uk

Addresses for companies within
The Random House Group Limited can be found at:
www.randomhouse.co.uk/offices.htm

The Random House Group Limited Reg. No. 954009

A CIP catalogue record for this book
is available from the British Library

ISBN 9780091900069

The Random House Group Limited supports The Forest Stewardship
Council® (FSC®), the leading international forest-certification organisation.
Our books carrying the FSC label are printed on FSC®-certified paper.
FSC is the only forest-certification scheme supported by the leading
environmental organisations, including Greenpeace. Our
paper procurement policy can be found at
www.randomhouse.co.uk/environment

MIX
Paper from
responsible sources
FSC® C016897

Printed and bound in Great Britain by Clays Ltd, St Ives plc

Contents

Contents

Introduction

This is not a book about 'taming', 'compliance' and 'perfect behaviours'. Rather, *Beyond Toddlerdom Tips* is about relationships: the art of keeping parents close and in love with their children.

Parents can either seize the moment and enjoy their children now or put it off forever. And I'm not talking about 'quality time', a trendy term that I hate with a passion. 'Quality time' implies small allocations of a parent's busy diary that is almost like a weekly appointment with a therapist. In fact, there is no such thing unless it tunes into a child's needs.

As I look back on the time I have spent with my own children, I have some regrets. I gave quality time but, as a busy paediatrician, it was usually on my terms. My youngest son had a fabulous kite, which we loved to fly together. He often asked, but usually on occasions when I was too busy. When I had time, there was no wind. The kite has long since disintegrated as has an opportunity that will not return.

Beyond Toddlerdom Tips enlists us as parents to treat our children the way we would like to be treated ourselves.

But *Beyond Toddlerdom Tips* is exactly that: my *top tips* for encouraging better behaviour in the five to twelves. If you would like more detailed information after reading this book, please move on to *Beyond Toddlerdom*.

Put simply, if we can take the time to stop, let the unimportant pass, always start with a clean slate, and most important of all, catch our children being good, the rest usually falls into place.

PART ONE

PART ONE

ONE

The Secrets of
Successful Parenting

I learnt the ideas you will read in this book from the thousands of parents and children I have attempted to help every day in my work. I don't pretend to have all the answers, but based on more than twenty-five years' experience, here are my top fifteen secrets of successful parenting.

1. Be available

Children need a parent who is available to sit, listen, do things together and marvel at what they see.

2. Routine and structure

Chaos makes us all feel as if we've got no control over the situation. Like adults, children are happiest when they know what's coming next.

3. Consistent limits and rules

Children are at their most secure when they know the rules and how far they can push those limits.

Children may protest our limits but at least they know we care enough to care what they do.

4. Flexibility and compromise

Parents need to adjust the rules to fit the individual situation: children must tidy away the dinner dishes, but tonight there is so much homework they can be excused.

5. Choice and freedom

While a two-year-old can't cope with choice, a school-age child needs some freedom to decide their own destiny. If it must be tuna and beetroot sandwiches every day, it's their choice.

6. Communicate clearly

To gain a child's attention, look them directly in the eye, talk simply and speak as though you mean it. Show them you're interested.

If you wish a child to respond, address them with interest and enthusiasm.

7. Ask, don't nag

The more you nag, the more obstinate and angry children

Children switch off and go deaf when parents nag. become. Instead tell them what you wish them to do, encourage action, monitor results, then get off their backs.

8. Notice the good

When we work hard and others only notice our faults and not the effort, it's a sure way to discourage and dishearten.

Catch your children being good. Let children know when you are pleased. Change the focus from only seeing the bad.

9. Reward good behaviour

The rock concert has been spectacular and you wish it would never end. As the last note fades the audience springs to their feet and shrieks their appreciation. The band responds to this show of enthusiasm and plays two more numbers.

The audience rewarded the band for their good

playing. The band rewarded the audience for their enthusiasm. This was a win–win situation.

Similarly, we mould our children's behaviour by ensuring the right (not the wrong) actions pay off.

10. Subtle rewards are the best

Soft, subtle encouragement is the most powerful way to boost behaviour. Children know they are doing well by the way we look at them, the twinkle in our eyes, our tone of voice, our level of interest and the gentle reassuring touch as we brush by.

11. Confrontation causes resentment

Children don't like being steamrollered and bullied: 'Just shut up and do it'. This heavy form of discipline would bring out the worst in any of us. We would resent the confrontation and feel angry and drag our feet.

12. Calm spreads calm

If parents can keep calm, children are easier to control. Even the sweetest child can be intensely irritating, but successful parents don't escalate by adding heat to an already overheated situation. They communicate in a calm voice, repeat their request like a broken record and move away before they lose their cool.

13. Cool off and regain control

Your German shepherd guard dog has an attitude problem. In the park he starts a skirmish with a psychopathic sheepdog. As the hair flies, do you issue polite instructions such as 'Sit, Fritz', or 'Lassie, heel'?

When we are in the midst of a dogfight, the first priority is to separate and reduce the heat. Once calm is re-established, rules and discipline can return.

14. Forgive and move on

Be a peace maker. After anger or punishment, forgive fast and start afresh with a clean slate. Be a peace maker. If at first your efforts are not accepted, keep offering the olive branch.

15. Don't stir up the animals

When working in the lions' cage, do you take a stick and poke them in the backside or do you tread gently and avoid trouble?

Let the unimportant things pass.

Some parents nitpick and escalate every trivial event. They are incapable of letting an unimportant behaviour pass. We don't want to let our children get away with murder, but it isn't clever to stir up the animals over every imperfection.

TWO

How Five to Twelves Think, Feel and Behave

The way five- to twelve-year-olds think, feel and behave is far more complicated than toddlers, who only have one problem: a serious lack of sense. But school-age children regularly make parents wonder if *they* are the ones who lack the sense.

Luckily, you need not feel that you are losing your marbles permanently. School-age children are easier to understand once you realise that they go through two very different stages of development during these years: the dependent and innocent stage between the five and eight years, and the much more independent and grown-up stage between eight and twelve.

School-age children go through two very different stages of development.

The five- to eight-year-old

These little people still carry much of the unspoiled innocence of the preschool years. They remain close and immensely dependent on their mum and dad. They are cuddly, uncomplicated and usually keen to please. They skip, effervesce and believe in ghosts and monsters.

They seem so grown up as they stride off in their new school uniform. They can sit, concentrate, mix, communicate clearly and write and read some words. But don't be fooled by this superficial show of maturity, because the five-year-old is still a baby in many ways.

Total dependence

Little children may appear to ignore what we say, but behind this pretence they watch what we do and tune into our beliefs and values. Even your words get recycled. As you hear them talk to their friends, they might sound like you on a bad day: 'I'm tired of having to tell you!'; 'I don't think I can play. I feel a headache coming on.' Other children and teachers may

If Dad believes the greenhouse effect is caused by cattle passing wind, there's no debate, it's cows farting that does it.

seed some ideas in their minds, but we parents are still the main source of wisdom. For these few years you are seen as infallible. Enjoy this brief moment of power, because it passes all too quickly!

A magic mind

Six-year-olds are fitted with a technicolour imagination. They don't really believe in ghosts and monsters, but when the night is very dark, they worry that something

13

might be out there. Fact and fiction can also get blurred and it's important to be aware of imaginative exaggeration. If your six-year-old makes claims about his teacher, the story you hear may not be the complete truth. It is wise to first check the facts before you round up a posse for a shoot-out with the principal.

The age of innocence

This is a wonderful time when children don't just walk: they skip, wave their arms and bounce with enthusiasm. It is also a magic time when children sit on your knee and snuggle up close. If it's cuddles you are after, this is the age to get your share.

Six-year-olds know nothing of apples, serpents and Original Sin.

And young children are unfazed by nudity. A six-year-old will race around the house wearing nothing more than a whoop of joy. At this age they do what feels right and their minds are unpolluted by adult shame and modesty.

Open and helpful

Seven-year-olds are remarkably up front, and if you listen you will hear most of what's on their minds. Such is their openness they can't keep a secret, so when they buy your birthday present they have to drop hints – they can't wait until the big day. Make the most of this forthrightness to establish clear lines of communication at this time because, as they get older, they will be less open.

Too honest

Under-eights know nothing of political correctness. They call things as they see them. So when a five-year-old spots a fat lady or a one-legged man, they will announce it to the world. Even when they pass wind, they apologise politely rather than disown the noise.

Love rules and regulations

Six-year-olds enjoy the clear structure of school, where they work quietly and raise a hand before they speak. At this young age, classroom regulations are like commandments delivered on tablets from the mount.

Six-year-olds also like to see the rules obeyed: 'Please Miss, Jack took Sarah's pencil'. But this time of informing on others is short-lived, and by the age of seven or eight it's already uncool to tell on your mates.

Value is a fuzzy notion

The under-eight has little idea about money or property. If the ball they kick shatters a priceless vase, it is Mum's anger, not the monetary value, that catches their attention.

Some infant teachers joke that they should do a strip search at going home time. Though most children are reasonably honest, under-eights are also often fitted with remarkably light fingers, as pencils, toys and trinkets seem to just slip into pockets.

This immaturity with money and ownership is all part of growing up. Our response at this age should be low key: just state what you believe happened, register your disapproval and watch out for repetitions.

Lives for the present

A five-year-old has no appreciation of the long-term future. We might explain a complex idea to our under-eights but they won't really understand: 'Grandma got sick with pneumonia, went to hospital, died and is now in heaven'.

They can repeat this, but have no understanding of pneumonia, heaven or death and can't grasp the

16

permanent nature of this event. To them Grandma is on a long holiday and may well come back.

Unspoken worries

Psychiatrists are continually amazed at how five- to eight-year-olds can grasp the wrong end of the stick then worry themselves silly over unimportant things.

As a young child, I was always warned about the dangers of germs. At that time we lived near a large hospital for infectious diseases that was surrounded by a high wall. Every time my parents drove past it I crouched low in the back of the car and held my breath to protect myself from any germ that might vault over the wall and land on me. But they never knew that this was troubling me: they just wondered why I was blue and breathless.

Little minds may worry more than we think.

Similarity of boys and girls

While girls are generally more verbal and boys may have more behaviour and learning problems, at this age boys and girls are more similar than they ever will be again.

Both boys and girls wonder about their anatomical differences, but this is an innocent interest without any sexual overtones. At this age boys more often play with boys and girls with girls, but it's okay to mix.

However, after the age of eight years, growth, development and maturity race ahead, and with this comes a definite segregation of the sexes.

The eight- to twelve-year-old

At eight years, children are increasingly influenced by teachers, school friends, the media and their environment, and they start to question their parents' values and wisdom.

Children of this age compare their looks, school performance, social acceptance and sporting abilities, then become worried when they don't match up. Cuddles become rare, and now only babies believe in monsters.

Parents out of power

By the time our child is eight, all our words and actions come into question.

Before, you could just lay down the law: 'Because I say so!' Now, you will get poor compliance without some explanation and good reason. Teachers are never wrong, but mothers often are! This shift of power takes many parents by surprise.

It was never mentioned in the owner's manual: you thought that parents were always in charge! Now you're not so sure.

The influence of others

Parents lose their monopoly as other people exert their influence. The soccer coach talks about the dangers of smoking so John confronts his puffing dad about fitness, heart attacks and toes dropping off. We have spent eight years teaching politeness, manners and healthy eating, and now the influence of their mates dismantles much of our hard work.

This can be a strange time for parents, when we see less of our children and know they are being influenced by others.

A long-term view of life

An eight-year-old's view of life is strictly in the here and now. But after eight they look into the distance and can see the permanent nature of events.

The silly worries of the younger child have disappeared, but they are replaced by the usual insecurities, fears and paranoia that trouble most people between the age of eight and eighty years.

Competes and compares

The young child will breeze along, not too concerned by their differences and difficulties. But at eight, they start to worry about how others see them.

We can tell our children they are bright, good-looking and wonderful, but they still match themselves against the group. They feel inadequate when they don't make the grade, and with this can come problems of esteem.

A loss of innocence

After the age of eight, Santa is silly and skipping is for babies. And the only time you will get a cuddle may be when they are almost asleep, 98 per cent unconscious and unable to resist.

If you open the door on a naked nine-year-old they cover everything and protest. The once uncomplicated mind has matured to a more adult plane.

One mother opened her washing machine to find it white with tissues. 'Who left these in their pockets?' she asked.

Her nine-year-old looked her in the eyes and replied, 'It couldn't have been me. You know I only use my sleeve.'

The school-age smart arse

Beware! From now on it's best to avoid arguments, as grown-ups will rarely win.

Children can make a nonsense out of our attempts to be serious.

They are also perfecting the art of put-downs. You make some earth-shattering observation to which they respond, with a yawn, 'Fascinating, Dad'. Soon you are told your jokes aren't funny, then your taste in music is geriatric – and that's just the start.

School learning and language

Learning takes a giant leap forward during these years. The average six-year-old can read single words; by twelve, they can manage simple newspapers and almost this book. For eight- to twelve-year-olds, school is so important that those who have a learning weakness or who can't stick at a task are hurt by failure and suffer in esteem.

The use and understanding of language increases with age. At six years they can cope with a simple concept, for example, 'Why does the sign on the petrol pump say "No Smoking"?' By eight years they understand more complex questions and by twelve years they are fully versed in innuendo, double meaning and the subtle differences that come with a change in tone.

Segregation of the sexes

The boys often hunt in packs and don't welcome children who are different or out of step. Girls usually play two or three together and are generally more accepting of those who are shy or less popular.

The segregation that starts around eight remains an uneasy part of life until, in adolescence, boys and girls reunite in a more individual way.

THREE

Why Children Behave Badly

Fascinating

Any parent knows that children are not created equal in their behaviour and temperament. Rather, a child's behaviour is believed to be a mix of four influences. Each child starts with a very individual genetic **temperament**, part of which arrives out of the blue and part of which comes from Mum and Dad. This unique package of temperament is then uplifted or depressed by the actions of us, their **parents**. It is further altered by **security or stress** in the child's living environment. Finally, behaviour is driven by the wish for **attention**.

Temperament

Temperament is the foundation on which we parents build our eighteen-year-long construction project.

Variations in children's temperaments are immense. They are pre-programmed at birth. Look at a tiny infant of three months of age and, even at this early stage, you can start to see what joys lie ahead: easy-going, dreamy, clingy, demanding and explosive.

Temperaments: the statistics

In the preschool years it is estimated that about 40 per cent of children have a relatively easy temperament,

35 per cent are on middle ground, 15 per cent are quite difficult and 10 per cent are going to be a challenge.

Follow-up studies suggest that this carries through school age with reasonable con-sistency. If this is true, we can expect that roughly one-third of children will be a breeze, one-third will be manageable and one-tenth will visibly age their parents.

Let's be honest: there are some extremely challenging children out there.

Who creates temperament?

Mothers sometimes ask me with wide-eyed innocence, 'How did I get such an active, non-stop child?' As she talks I watch Dad rock, fidget, jiggle and become dis-tracted by what's outside the window. An out-of-step child can arrive out of the blue, but often you don't need to look far to see where they came from.

Troublesome temperaments

I mention difficult temperament not to depress parents but to explain the differences. Even if you have scored an easy, compliant child, don't get too smug because your luck may not hold out forever. If you have a child with a difficult temperament, don't take it personally: this is when the parenting techniques of this book will be put to the test.

Parenting style

I can't overestimate the importance of getting attitudes right at the start. When children are treated nicely, they treat you nicely. When children know they are loved, they let you know they love you.

When children set out on the rails, they generally stay on the rails.

Without positive parenting, nothing will work well. I don't tame children, I change parents, who then get the best out of their individual child.

Reaction to stress and uncertainty

Young children have super-sensitive antennae which pick up on upset and translate it back as a change in behaviour.

Never underestimate the effect of stress, change or parental unhappiness on a child. The child may not always understand what is going on around them, but they are acutely aware of any tension.

Positive parents:

- Communicate warmly with and without words.

- Listen, take time and enjoy doing things with their children.

- Mould good behaviour through encouragement and reward.

- Forgive quickly and hold no grudges.

- Transmit instructions with the expectation that things will happen.

- Watch with interest and pride.

- Keep their humour and their perspective.

- Focus on the good. Even the worst-behaved child is good for 90 per cent of the time.

Most commonly, a child will react to tension by becoming unsettled and ill at ease: they have a vague restlessness, seem unavailable, have upset sleep or their performance at school suffers. Whatever the reaction, whether it is restlessness, anger, clinging or withdrawal, these children are shouting at the top of their voices, 'I don't know what you are doing but it hurts!'

27

For children under the age of eight years, parental problems cause most pain. After this age, children react to troubles at school, problems mixing, learning difficulties and worries about the world. A few children show their stress by withdrawal. The child feels ill at ease, becomes solitary and quiet and loses enthusiasm for their usual activities.

Attention

Whatever a child's temperament, the parenting style or the living environment, annoying behaviour is always to do with gaining attention and power. The main way parents and teachers mould behaviour is through the giving and withdrawing of attention.

Every child loves to receive good attention, but when this is not on offer, they will try to attract any sort of attention that's going. Say Mum and Dad are having an important discussion. John feels excluded from their attention and tries to get in on the act. He asks a question but this is ignored. He interrupts and is pushed aside. Now he turns on the TV, torments the dog and

The giving and taking of attention is the basic principle of effective discipline.

imitates fart sounds. Mum and Dad become intensely irritated, close the conversation and John is rewarded with 100 per cent attention. This is poor-quality attention, but it's better than being ignored.

We shape our children's behaviour by boosting the good patterns with attention and reward while discouraging the bad by pulling back on our attention.

FOUR

Positive Discipline

There is one important principle that steers our children's behaviour: a behaviour that pays off for the child will usually be repeated; a behaviour that does not pay off will disappear. This is the basic rule that allows parents to increase the good and decrease the bad. All it takes is a wise choice as to the behaviours that pay off. The pay-offs we use are soft rewards, hard rewards, and cumulative rewards.

Soft rewards

Never underestimate the power of soft and subtle pay-offs, especially when it comes to children. These are the most important rewards. Catch your children being good, show them you mean it in your body language and tone of voice, and be specific in your praise. Though these

Dining at a top Sydney restaurant, the food and service were so good I called the head waiter over. Later, with an expectant smile, he approached and handed me the bill. My wife suggested I should leave a large tip, so I explained to her about soft and hard rewards. She listened then summed up quite simply: 'Interesting, but you are still cheap and mean.' My wife was probably right.

rewards are of most importance to the under-fives, their influence is immense right through life.

Soft rewards include enthusiasm, encouragement, noticing, words, body language and tone of voice.

Catch them being good

One of the greatest traps for parents is to become so negative that we see nothing but the bad. Positive parents turn this around and use their words to boost the good: 'I like it when you both play so well', 'Gosh, you were such a help at the supermarket'; 'Have the cleaners been here?'.

The power of body language

We sense genuine interest by attitude and body language. Children also know we are pleased by the tone of our voice, the way we look, the twinkle in our eye and the things we whisper. This subtle form of encouragement is one of the most powerful tools of discipline.

Be specific

School-age children are unmoved by unfocused, over-used encouragement. We blandly say, 'Good girl', 'Well done', 'Clever boy', which is about as genuine as the parrot who announces, 'Who's a pretty boy?' Older children may even react badly to these unfocused comments and turn our words back on us: we say, 'That's good' and they reply, 'No, it sucks'; 'You're looking great' – 'No, I'm not'; 'I like your story' – 'No, it's boring.'

Make your encouragement specific. 'Gosh, this room is not only tidy, you've even polished your desk'; 'In your story, I like the boy character who saved the ship'; 'I really like the way the sun lights up this side of your painting.'

Hard rewards

Now we are entering the real world where people encourage action through gifts, favours, privileges, money and bribes. Hard rewards are particularly useful for the older child.

Hard rewards include time, privileges, food or other treats and money.

Some experts get their knickers in a twist debating the difference between rewards and bribes. A *reward* comes as a bonus after the event and consolidates a good behaviour. A *bribe* is arranged beforehand and if there is no performance there is no payout. We all prefer to use rewards rather than bribes, but sometimes the difference is academic.

34

When I set up a behaviour program with parents, we first list the rewards that are likely to grab their child's interest. As parents we must find the magic motivator for our child. If we don't tailor our program to the individual, what follows will always fall flat.

If what you are doing works, just call it a reward and we'll all be happy.

The most effective rewards for eight- to twelve-year-olds are:

Time

We often forget that time is one of our most valuable possessions and is also one of our most appreciated rewards. Your son has stuck at his homework and done it well: 'Fancy going for a splash down in the pool?'; 'Would you like me to run you over to Steve's house?'

Privileges

These are great motivators for the six- to eighteen-year-old. When things have gone well, they are allowed some extra bit of the action. This may be time on the telephone, more television, a later bed time, access to the computer, being excused from doing a usual chore, choosing dinner, having a friend to stay, picking where you go for a meal out.

Food

It may come as a disappointment to the animal admirers, but sea lions don't do tricks because they like to impress

Purists dislike the idea of bribing children with stuff that rots teeth, but this technique has been popular since it was first invented by grandmothers.

humans. They perform because each action is rewarded with a mouthful of raw fish. People may object, but if food works for all other animal trainers, it must be worth a try with children.

Of course, we can reward with the healthiest of health foods, but children tend to value these less than foods high in sugar, preservatives, additives, colours and flavours, especially if they come with the latest in movie merchandise.

Food is mostly a motivator with the under-eights, but it can focus interest at any age. (I for one can always be bought by the offer of a good meal.) With your children, don't go over the top but if some mouth-watering snack tunes in the obedience antennae, it can't be all that bad.

Money

This may be the root of all evil, but it sure grabs the attention of some children.

So a productivity bonus should be capped at an appropriate level. Small cash payments can be varied and mixed with other

There is one major drawback when you reward with money: it leaves you open to extortion.

rewards to prevent them becoming a God-given right.

Cumulative rewards

As children get older, they can appreciate rewards that are more abstract and less immediate. Now they can visualise the payout from stars or tokens.

Cumulative rewards include star charts, tokens, points.

Star charts

Stars allow us to focus a child's attention on specific behaviours that need to be changed. The chart is a simple piece of paper. The column on the left-hand margin lists the days of the week and the row across the top, the behaviours we wish to target. Each time the behaviour

Stars only work with children who are old enough to recognise what they represent. They have no meaning for the under-fours.

is achieved we stick a star in the appropriate square. If there is compliance, soon a galaxy of stars illuminates the page and this is rewarded with some prearranged payout. The chart is put in a place of prominence, usually stuck to the fridge door. As fridges are opened continually, the average child can monitor their progress throughout the day.

The targets we star must be clear cut and easily achievable. It's pointless expecting a child to 'be good all day', or to 'not annoy your sister'. A turnaround of this magnitude is reserved for faith healers, miracle workers and saints.

Warning: stars create maximum interest in the first week, less in the second and soon the star burns out, leaving a black hole.

I use stars to highlight two or more simple behaviours; for example, brushes teeth, makes bed, does dishes, ready for school on time. Stars can also be used when there are problems of daytime bladder training.

The token system

This is a popular technique that takes an impossibly big task and divides it into small manageable units. It is based on the same principle as my Frequent Flyer points. My favourite airline wishes to encourage a certain behaviour (loyalty to Qantas) so I receive points each time I fly. After a year of this correct behaviour I get a special treat, like a holiday in Alice Springs.

Tokens won't turn a terrorist into an angel, but they are more appropriate than deep sedation or a straitjacket.

For instance, many parents dread the drama of long-distance car travel. You buy books, CDs and games but the pain continues. Now try a token system. For every fifteen minutes of peace a token is dropped in a cup and this adds up to a payout of money or a special treat at the next fuel stop.

Punishment without Pain

By this point in the book it will be clear that discipline is based on encouragement and reward. There is, however, a small place for punishment, but it is punishment without pain. We don't hit or hurt children. Instead we punish using things like:

- our tone of voice;

- switching off attention;

- active ignoring;

- time out;

- withdrawing privileges; and

- penalities (that encourage the positive).

The tone of disapproval

If your poodle piddles on the carpet or your basset barks all night, who are you going to call? Bark Busters! And these dog trainers will start by telling you, 'Use fewer words, but more tone'. You don't explain to your barking dog that your neighbour is on Prozac for a nervous disorder and it would be good if he kept quiet. You look him in the eye and sternly say, 'Bah!'

Now, I am not suggesting we get Bark Busters to sort

out our children, but tone transmits more message than a whole chapter of carefully chosen words.

Switching off attention

Children thrive when they live in a home filled with interest and interaction, where they get plenty of positive attention. We know that giving attention is the greatest reward, so it follows that cutting attention is a potent punishment.

A six-year-old is being tickled and bounced on Mum's knee. In a burst of innocent enthusiasm he head-butts Mum in the mouth. As the pain rises you could explode or explain the dangers of horseplay. But it is more effective to briefly register your hurt then walk away. The child feels the cool change from full attention to total ignoring. This registers your disapproval and will encourage more care the next time.

Active ignoring

Active ignoring allows us to take a step sideways yet remain in control. With this technique, you stay calm, make your point, disengage and then return.

The ten-year-old stands nose to nose, daring Mum to

When a defiant child is hellbent on confrontation, it's a hard call to ignore.

discipline. You quietly repeat your request, walk away, straighten the curtains, pour yourself a cup of coffee, then return to restate your position in a matter-of-fact way. Active ignoring sidesteps a stand-off, gives space and signals that we are not going to be manipulated.

Time out

This is one of the most useful weapons in our armoury. Time out punishes by withdrawing positive attention

Time out allows us to put a lid on escalation and to sidestep a stand-off.

from the child, then it provides the space to cool off an overheated situation. Time out is effective from age one to eleven years.

The young child is moved calmly to a bedroom or a time-out chair. Older children are expected to take themselves. The period of exclusion is calculated as approximately one minute for each year of age, but parents have to find the time that best suits their child.

■ Time out is signalled by a statement, a sign or taking

the five-year-old by the hand. If they refuse we move to plan B and use techniques such as counting to three, active ignoring or giving a choice.

■ Once in time out, if they call out, this is ignored. If they ask whether the time is up, don't rise to the bait – set a cooking timer and let it be the adjudicator. If they come out early, the clock goes back to the start.

■ At the end of time out, briefly restate your case but don't heap guilt or demand an apology. Then forgive fully and start afresh with a clean slate.

Another use of time out is to withhold toys, television and computers from feuding children who won't share. Jack wants 'The Simpsons', Jill wants 'Home and Away', and as they squabble no one sees anything. Mum issues a warning, then the television is put in time out. Switch off the set, start the cooking timer and when fifteen minutes is up, start again.

Withdrawing privileges

Good behaviour is rewarded with privileges and older children can be punished by the removal of privileges. Removing privileges can make children angry, so when removing privileges keep it fair and keep it short. They might miss the first half of a TV program, have no television or telephone that night, no dessert or bedtime comes half an hour earlier.

Removing privileges is effective, but never issue a threat you are not prepared to carry through. It's pointless saying, 'I'll cancel your party', when the cake is bought, friends are being scrubbed up ready to attend and you have no real intention of pulling the plug.

Penalties

Every day my life is a minefield of consequences and penalties. I don't put petrol in my car – I have to walk to work. I drive too fast – I get a speeding ticket. I annoy the butcher – I get tough meat.

Consequences are part of life, and school-age children need to understand them. You don't wear your bike helmet – the bike is locked up for two weeks. You don't brush your teeth – lollies are banned and water is your drink. You stick chewing gum on the dog – no gum in the house for one month.

Beware: human beings get mighty stroppy when you start taking their stuff.

Penalties are slightly different: they usually involve removing possessions or money.

One penalty technique that encourages the positive is to start with ten points, then add two for the good and deduct one for the bad. With this, it's hard to hit a negative balance.

The three-strikes system

The three-strikes system is used by some schools. A disruptive child starts each class with three lives. These can be shown as three cardboard stars sitting on the desk, a tally on the edge of the blackboard or three strokes on a sheet of paper. For each indiscretion, one life is quietly removed. If there are none left at the end of the lesson, they must sit for five minutes before release.

Does smacking work?

There are much better ways to discipline and force leads to greater problems. There is no place for punishment with pain.

In easy kids, smacking may get some response, but so do all the other techniques, so it is unnecessary.

47

Smacking doesn't work and it can be downright dangerous because it can lead to escalation.

Besides, when do you stop smacking? Do you wait until they are bigger, quicker or more violent than you? And then what's the alternative?

I don't support the groups who wish to imprison parents and teachers who smack, but it does not mean I encourage violence. School-age children should not be smacked.

48

S I X

Help for Behaviour Problems

When parents come to me, many are in a state of numb confusion. They are quite clear that they don't like what is going on, but they can't see why it's happening.

My first priority is to find the true nature of the problem. How much of the difficulty is in the child? What stresses are stirring the environment? There are a number of simple methods to cut through the confusion.

The magic wand

When parents are asked, 'What's the problem?' they often are so stressed they answer, 'Everything!' Only a miracle worker can sort out 'everything'. I can only deal in specifics.

To help narrow the focus I ask, 'If I had a magic wand and could only change one bit of behaviour, what would that be?' When I get that answer, I then ask, 'If you had a second wish, what is the next most troublesome behaviour?'

If you think your child has a behaviour problem, first try the magic wand to pinpoint what's bothering you.

The magic wand helps parents think more clearly and shows me what I must target. Mums often see things differently to dads, but both know what is causing them pain.

Describe a day

Children can be irritating and obnoxious at home, then act like angels in my office. Parents worry that I won't believe their story and secretly hope the child will be abusive and trash my room. Even the worst-behaved child can make you look a liar in a non-confronting interview situation. To get around this I get the parents to take me through the typical day.

What time does she wake? Is she usually in good form? What happens between getting up and breakfast time? I then go through the day, getting a technicolour picture of every moment. I want to hear about the usual day, not the worst-case scenario. Armed with this information I then can begin to help.

Keep a behaviour diary

A good psychologist will usually start by asking parents to keep a behaviour diary. This measures the frequency, severity and duration of all behaviour, good and bad. From this baseline the psychologist documents the reality of what is happening and can then see when the techniques they suggest are creating change.

It is useful to write down exactly what is going on as our perception can be very unreliable.

Don't over-analyse

I meet some parents whose child's every action is interpreted as having some deep significance. An ornament gets bumped by an exuberant child and this is analysed as a deliberate act of destruction. An impulsive outburst is seen as premeditated aggression. Even teasing their sister is labelled spiteful jealousy. Our job is to help parents change to a happy relationship, not to over-analyse their children.

Parents who over-interpret may blame incorrectly, become paranoid and miss the point.

The ABC approach

ABC is a simple way to sort out behaviour. Each problem is looked at in three parts:

A. The antecedent (what triggered it off).

B. The behaviour (what the child did).

C. The consequence (how we reacted and what were the pay-offs).

Putting ABC into action

'Lisa was in the lounge room watching a TV soap. I told her to switch off the set, to tidy away her toys, wash her hands and come to the table immediately. She ignored me. I turned off the television, she shouted at me and I lost it.'

Lisa dragged her feet, came to the table, grumbled throughout the meal, fiddled with her food and provoked all the way until bedtime.

How the disaster could have been handled

A. The antecedent

Lisa's television program had only eight minutes to run. Could she have waited until the next commercial or the end? Was it important to tidy the toys before dinner-time, or could that have happened later? If Lisa didn't eat her dinner, who was really going to miss out?

B. The behaviour

Was Mum committed to forgive or was she spoiling for a fight? Should Mum and her daughter have moved apart for a short time or even used time out?

It takes two people to keep a battle on the boil.

C. The consequence

Was it worth it? There were no winners, just losers. Things might have been different if there had been a warning, if Mum had waited until a commercial break, if Mum had resorted to less confrontation and had tried to stay calm, instead of stirring the conflict.

Finding the best behaviour technique

Life must be easy for those who write advice books but don't work with difficult children. By the time I meet parents, most have tried all the usual techniques and are still in trouble. I often look at the difficulties and wonder what more I can suggest. When faced with this I go back to basics. I review every possible method to see what brings some success, what is of little value and what is a total failure.

As a rule, shouting, nitpicking, confronting, arguing and escalating all make things worse. Rules, rewards, letting the unimportant pass, time out, keeping calm, 'I' statements and forgiveness give the best chance.

SEVEN

Tips for Starting School

In the years between five and twelve there is a massive explosion of knowledge. At the start a child can barely hold a pen, write their name, count past twenty or read a word. By their thirteenth birthday most write with style, perform complex calculation and read like an adult. All this comes from hours of effort by teachers, parents and children.

Skills for starting school

Social skills

Children need to: mix, share, play together, work in a group, sit and listen, use the toilet independently, have good behaviour control and the ability to separate from Mum.

Academic skills

Children should be able to: hold a pen, write their given name, recognise some letters, know numbers, count objects and have good receptive and spoken language.

To start early or hold back?

While the local law allows children to start education at four years, school enrolment is usually not compulsory until the age of five years. Young children vary greatly in their social and emotional maturity. Some are ripe for an early start, but others need more months to develop. Children must be socially ready, and preferably academically ready, at the start.

Those who encourage late enrolments note that mature starters have stronger self-esteem and more impressive leadership skills in later years. Some children who start before they are ready remain on the outer edge and never make it to centre stage.

If your child is eligible to start young, look carefully at their social readiness. Talk about next year with their preschool director. They know how your child compares with the others who are preparing for school. If the director says no, take it seriously.

Many parents have no choice as, for them, school provides the only affordable form of child care. But if you have concerns and finances will support it, take the safe option and hold back.

A late start will never do harm, but starting too soon can cause problems that don't go away.

The first day

Preparation is important. Talk about the school, try on the uniform, visit the class and participate in the orientation program. Be positive but be realistic – school is for education, not entertainment. School may cater for a lot of children but it's not Santa's Cave or Disneyland.

The start of school for a child is like arriving to take up a new job for an adult. It takes two months for an adult to feel comfortable, so do allow equal time for a child to settle.

Find out whether a child from preschool or the neighbourhood will be in your child's class and, if possible, ask them over during the holidays. Plan the food for little lunch and big lunch, but don't overcompensate with treats that rot their teeth and clog the arteries.

On the first day allow yourself plenty of time to avoid the pressure of a rush. Ensure there are no clashing appointments so that you can have as much time as it takes. Walk in with a positive stride, find the classroom, meet the class teacher, locate the toilets, put down the school bag and find a friend. Let your child know what is going to happen, when you are going to leave and the time you will be back. If there are any problems the teacher will tell you what to do. When junior is settled, depart decisively.

Home behaviour

As learning and playing consumes so much energy, excessive tiredness is almost universal among children starting school.

For many, school becomes so important they talk, think and play it all the time. Infant sisters, dogs, cats and anything that can sit will be commandeered to become part of their teacher–pupil games. Others would divulge nothing, even if the KGB were providing a prompt.

Some children start school with an enthusiasm that later drops sharply. Be supportive but firm about attendance.

Starting school is a major disruption to the stability of life, and behaviour that is normally good can slip off the straight and narrow. It's quite common for children just starting school to suddenly have unreliable bladders, unexpected clinginess, be defiant, or experience disturbed sleep and start coming to their parents' bed.

Worries about learning

At least one child in ten has some weakness in learning.

Most early concerns are just a lag in maturity that will come good with short-term help. For others, the difficulties will cause pain throughout the school years and into adulthood.

Be aware that learning problems can pass unnoticed and may only be looked into when a child opts out or expresses their frustration via bad behaviour.

As schools tend to give children the benefit of the doubt and allow time to settle, it is often the parents who will make the first move in asking for help. If you have the slightest concern talk to the class teacher. Ask direct questions about your child's abilities in general learning, reading, maths, independent work output, mixing and playground behaviour. Ask if they are middle of the class, above average or below average in each one of these.

Ask if any concerns should be taken further. When specialist assessment is required, all state schools can arrange direct access to their counsellor and private schools can arrange this through their own channels.

The help is out there, but it's often you, the parent, who needs to make the first move.

Good parent–teacher communication

At the start of school make a commitment to keep in touch with the class teacher. It's unfair to ambush a tired teacher every day and expect an in-depth consultation, but a lack of involvement may be interpreted as a lack of interest. It's best to take a mid-position: not too pushy but make sure you know what's happening. Aim to touch base every two weeks. Just ask, 'Is everything okay? Is there anything I can do to help?'

Establish a close and respectful relationship with your child's teacher right from the start.

You spend five years getting close and supporting, nurturing and immersing your child in the values of your family. Then, at the start of school, the innocent Christian is cast to the lions.

There is no doubt that they will meet teasing, spite, drag-downs and bad language, but the home foundation will always remain the strongest influence. If we prepare our children properly and keep the family foundations strong, no Darth Vader will turn them to the dark side.

EIGHT
Sibling Squabbles

One day I was watching nature enthusiast David Attenborough on television when he unlocked one of the great mysteries of life. In his hesitant tones I heard the answer to why brothers and sisters squabble:

> 'It seems that all little animals (with the exception of hedgehogs) love to trip, roll and fight. This quickens their reflexes, tones up their bodies and prepares them for life in the wild. A little lion that fights with his brother or sister is more likely to survive in the hostile adult world.'

Now, I am not suggesting we encourage teasing and squabbles, but it probably has some residual benefit. Athletic strength is built on all those taunts, tumbles and fights. Verbal sparring tunes woolly words into a razor-sharp response. Sisters who cope with an annoying brother will be better prepared for an irritating man in their later life.

Why siblings fight
Related but not identical

My brother always wanted to be an only child. It's not that I am particularly painful; we are just very different people. As he sat with his head in a book, I wanted to be out inhaling fresh air. My school achievements were average, despite hours of study and homework. He worked for ten minutes each night then won every prize and scholarship. We have always been emotionally close, but we are very different people.

Parents fall into the trap believing all brothers and sisters will have identical personalities and interests. For their convenience the parents encourage different children to do the same activities, which may not suit. The message for parents is to use no one program, or no fixed expectation for all.

Even identical twins are not identical.

Attention and boredom

Analysts interpret skirmishing as an unresolved power struggle, but most squabbles are due to boredom. Life slips into a quiet patch and a taunt generates a power surge of attention.

The one who complains loudest is usually the most guilty.

It is tempting for parents to rush in like the United Nations at the first sign of trouble. They ask who started the fight and each child points at the other. Intervening may bring peace in the short term, but by rewarding with attention it encourages further fights. Parents must realise that a fight includes two combatants, and it's often hard to separate the good guys from the bad.

After the age of twelve years, words become the main weapon. 'Is that a dress or a tent?'; 'Have you ever wondered if you were adopted?'

Life's not fair

The early school years are a time of competition, complaints and that constant cry, 'It's not fair, Mum!' Avoid being intimidated by comparative justice: 'When Jan was eight, you bought her a new bike'; 'Jack does fewer chores but gets the same pocket money as me'.

Equality is a worthy but impractical goal. You may love your children equally, but they will not end up with the same amount of attention.

The demanding, dissatisfied, intrusive child always insists on more of our time. In life it is always the one who shouts loudest who gets most. The sensible parents go for peace before equality.

Don't get into debates about justice – you will never win.

When told, 'It's not fair, she got more', acknowledge the statement but don't enter into the argument.

How to cope with sibling fights
Establish limits

Setting limits won't stop squabbles, but they let the combatants know where they stand. Rules should cover ownership, the use of joint property, personal space and acceptable behaviour. Join the Marquess of Queensberry and set down your rules for the ring, such as:

- This shelf is for your sister's treasures. It is totally out of bounds.

- This bedroom is personal space. It cannot be entered without an invitation.

- No disturbances are ever permitted during homework time.

- Broken belongings will be paid for from pocket money or one of your good toys will be offered in exchange.

- At dinner time there will be no touching, insulting or kicking your brother.

Top ten tips for a peaceful life

1. Ignore minor squabbles.

2. Keep bored bodies busy.

3. Encourage co-operation by interesting the squabblers in a joint project.

4. Suggest they move their battle outside or to another room.

5. Give feedback for good co-operation: 'I love to see you two playing so well together.'

6. Give stars and tokens for squabble-free hours.

7. Put the disputed toy, computer or television in time out.

8. The child who complains about getting hurt should be advised to keep clear of trouble.

9. Don't interpret and apportion blame; just describe what you see and say what you will not accept.

10. When nothing works punish both with time out in different rooms.

Encouraging conflict resolution

It's easy to become a referee in our children's battles but it is better they develop the basics of conflict resolution. Here's how to help them:

- When hit with complaints, don't adjudicate. Ask, 'How can we resolve this problem?'

- Suggest some options.

- Say you will come back in one minute to hear their solution, otherwise send to time out.

Take the peaceful path

When siblings fight, parents have two options: to take the confronting path or the peaceful path. Some cynics suggest the complete ignoring approach: no parental intervention unless there is blood on the carpet. It doesn't have to be this extreme, but I still support the laid-back approach.

Note: Occasionally one child is unacceptably vindictive or resentful to a sibling. This is more than normal sibling rivalry, and needs professional intervention.

NINE

Increasing Self-esteem

Self-esteem is how a child feels about themselves. When self-esteem is high, they are likely to be confident, positive, sociable, kind to others and more willing to attempt new tasks. When it is low, children may be negative, withdrawn, socially insecure and can even be quite paranoid.

Self-esteem rises with stability, close support, a trusted confidant and the feeling of belonging.

It's bad enough worrying about non-problems, but when there are genuine concerns about ability, appearance, body size or social skills, a child may distort these way out of all proportion.

Encouraging self-esteem

While there is no easy way of boosting a child's self-esteem, there are things we can do to help.

Start early

Esteem is not something that develops at the age of six. Its foundation is laid in the toddler years. Young children are intensely dependent on their parents, and if we treat them as special, they feel special. But it takes more than having us around to boost esteem – we also need to be available. Littlies need a listener, a comforter, a responder, an encourager, an audience and a safety net.

An unhurried grandparent has special powers that boost esteem. They listen in wonderment as their tongue-tied granddaughter rambles on, making the little person feel like a wit, a raconteur and a legend in their own lifetime. This early feeling of security and importance sets the foundation for better esteem.

Children do best when we listen, respect their feelings, appreciate effort and accept their mistakes.

Notice and listen

School-agers can ramble, lose the plot or wallow in such trivia your brain starts to ache. They talk of non-topics such as teenage pop groups or some program that would be better taken off the telly. But listening is important. If a child is to feel valuable, what they say should be valued. Show interest in their friends, work, hobbies, sports and words. Give feedback that lets them know you are with them.

Avoid bland generalities like 'Well done', 'That's good', 'You're

Let you children know they are worth listening to.

clever'. Pick up on specifics, such as 'I love the prince's blue eyes in your story', as this lets them know you have a genuine interest. If we tune in to what our children do and say, they realise they must be worth noticing.

Respect their fears and feelings

All of us have our problems and worries: some are quite genuine, others are largely in our head. You can comfort the anxious air traveller with safety statistics, but five miles up in turbulence you might as well be telling Leonardo DiCaprio that the *Titanic* is unsinkable.

Even the most successful, clever and attractive child may have a poor perception of themselves. Whether our worries are real or perceived, our bodies feel the same adrenalin upset and nothing others say will make much difference. School-age children may fear child abductors, germs, bullies, dirty toilets, the dark, spelling tests, talking in front of the class or being alone. It's not for us to reason why; our goal is to acknowledge, desensitise and give support to help them get on top. If we trivialise how a child feels, this affects their feeling of esteem.

Children should be accepted along with their fears,

feelings and frustrations. When they are upset with their results, let them know that they worked hard, then together work towards a better outcome next time.

It's okay to be wrong

The only people who don't do anything wrong are those who don't do anything. Children need to know that we all make mistakes. When a child makes a mistake or fears failure the problems appear bigger than they are and this eats away at their self-esteem. Children need to be encouraged to try, accepted when they fail and supported to try again. Explain that by making mistakes we learn from the process. Let them hear you say, 'I was wrong. I made a mistake. Next time I'll do it differently.'

Avoid words that wound

When parents are driven to the edge of mental destruction, it's easy to drop the nice talk and use words that wound: 'You've ruined it for all of us'; 'Grow up'; 'Just go away'; 'Don't be so stupid'.

Remember it is the behaviour, not the child, that we dislike.

Even when they are merciless in their assault, try to avoid using only negative words.

Use 'I' statements, not 'you' statements

Humans feel less criticised when they hear a statement about how you feel rather than how they annoy. So turn things around and say, 'I feel upset when we fight with each other'; 'I feel embarrassed when this happens in front of my friends'; 'I feel sad when I hear words like that'. Also avoid the chill of passive-aggression, where the words are okay but the intonation is laced with poison.

Give responsibility within reason

Children can be slow, messy, unreliable and wasteful, but if we don't let them do real tasks, they will never learn. We also need to avoid constantly using negative words: 'Don't slice the bread, you'll cut your finger'; 'Don't run, you'll trip'; 'Don't climb, you'll fall'. Instead, turn the sentence around: 'Hold the railing so you're safe'.

Aim for a balance between independence and safety. The aim is to let our children hold the controls and fly as co-pilots with the captain sitting close by. Children need to feel trusted if they are going to trust themselves.

There are no miracle methods to boost self-esteem, just commonsense suggestions: start early, notice, listen, show genuine interest, recognise effort, be specific in praise, watch your words, accept feelings, give responsibility, show trust, accept screw-ups and allow each child to savour success at something.

Help them savour success

Every child needs to feel they have talent. Some get a great boost from team sports, while the lone spirits enjoy running, cycling, swimming or ascending some far-off peak. Craft, music, computers, drama and clubs are useful outlets. The aim is to move away from what our children cannot do to what they can do. For children to gain confidence they need to savour success at something, and it's up to us to find what that something is.

Aim for confidence in the classroom

Teachers boost esteem by making each child feel they are important and belong. So the child who struggles gets the same responsibilities and privileges as the potential Rhodes Scholar.

For example, a child who is weak in one area or socially insecure can be asked to tutor other children in their area of strength. Many schools have a 'buddy system', where a mature older child guides and supports one less able. With schoolwork, attempts are appreciated, mistakes are accepted and effort is acknowledged.

T E N
Diet, Weight and Exercise

Until recently the word 'diet' meant a brief, painful period of deprivation. Now, the secret is to establish a

The key to good health that lasts a lifetime is to start early.

sensible diet, maintain appropriate weight and adopt a more active, fitter lifestyle from an early age. And to do it at a level that can be easily sustained over the next eighty years.

We can help set up our children for a healthy life by establishing a sensible and sustainable balance of diet, exercise and lifestyle at the earliest age.

A balanced diet

The energy that powers our children comes from the carbohydrates, fat and protein in food. Such is the metabolism of young children, they need all the zip they can get, and quite a bit must come from fat. After the age of two, they need to gradually change to the low-fat, high-carbohydrate diet of the health-conscious adult. But don't remove fat completely. For example, use low fat milk rather than skimmed milk. That way children will still have enough energy for growth and development.

Carbohydrates: quite complex

Carbohydrate is the main source of energy for parents,

footy players, athletes and children. It comes as simple, quickly digested sugars or the slower-released complex carbohydrate found in bread, breakfast cereals, pasta, rice and vegetables.

Complex carbohydrate foods contain varying amounts of dietary fibre. While fibre is not digested, it is vital to the long-term health of body and bowel.

Sugar is still sugar, whether it is called glucose, honey or molasses.

Within reason, children can eat unlimited amounts of complex carbohydrate without increasing the risk of obesity. However, highly refined sugars do require some restriction as they are easy to take in excess, which can easily turn to body fat. Sugars also damage teeth. In an ideal diet at least two-thirds of the carbohydrate should be in the complex form.

Beware of 'health bars': they may still contain high levels of fat (and sugars). Always read the label.

Fats

Today's new breed of cardiologist believes that the time to start preventing adult heart disease is not at the age of forty but in the early years. This is because studies have found that the earliest signs of coronary artery narrowing are commonly found in both young adults and adolescents. These fatty deposits in artery walls are laying down the foundation for future trouble.

The fat in our diet is intimately involved with the body's production of cholesterol. And cholesterol can cause the damage to arteries that causes heart disease.

A high total cholesterol is not necessarily a problem – it's the type of cholesterol that makes the difference.

When fats are broken down they may produce 'good' cholesterol – high-density cholesterol (HDL), which reduces the risk of artery damage. But they can also produce 'bad' cholesterol – low-density cholesterol (LDL), which greatly raises the risk of heart attack and stroke. Those with the best chance of maintaining healthy arteries either have a low level or an average LDL cholesterol, which is protected by a high HDL cholesterol.

The ability to lay down fat in the arteries has a strong hereditary link: certain families seem relatively immune despite their diet while others who take great care may still develop heart disease. We can't change our genes but we can improve our children's chances if we lower the LDL and raise the HDL levels of cholesterol.

'Good' fat (Polyunsaturated or monounsaturated fats)	'Bad' fat (Mainly saturated fat)
■ Most vegetable oils	■ Palm and coconut oil
■ Fish, especially tuna, salmon and sardines	■ Commercial cakes, biscuits and pastries
■ Peanuts, not pastes	■ Take-away fried foods
■ Some margarines	■ Fatty meats
	■ Full-fat dairy foods

Remember:

■ Saturated fat increases LDL (the 'bad' cholesterol).

■ Polyunsaturated fat decreases LDL but also HDL (the 'good' cholesterol).

■ Monounsaturated fats decrease 'bad' cholesterol but tend not to affect 'good' cholesterol.

Protein, iron and calcium

In general, a child will have the right nutritional balance if they regularly eat small portions of meat and have a substantial dairy intake. If the majority of a child's protein supply is coming from meat, it will bring with it an ample amount of the best quality of absorbable iron. Iron is needed to make haemoglobin, which carries oxygen in the blood.

Milk and dairy products provide most of our children's intake of calcium. Establishing a good calcium habit is essential, as the mineral we set down in the first half of our lives helps protects us against brittle bones (osteoporosis) in older years.

Fruits, vegetables and vitamins

Vitamins can come as packs of pills, or through nature, by eating a wide variety of fruit and vegetables. The natural way has the added advantage of providing trace elements, antioxidants and other essential micronutrients.

Since this is a chapter on health, not chemistry, I will spare you the finer technical details. The main point is that children between five and twelve years need to get interested in fruit and vegetables and the wider the variety the better. While all this might sound like 'grandma knows best', it is worth taking seriously. Of course, most parents would give up their superannuation to get their kids to salivate over vegetables.

Hints for increasing fruit and veg intake

Do:

- Offer fruit morning, noon and night -- and as snacks.

- Buy small amounts of many different kinds of fresh fruits and vegetables. Variety and freshness really help.

- Offer vegies at main meals -- even in small amounts.

- Add finely chopped vegetables to sauces and soups.

- Zip up the flavour by adding a little dressing to salads or a little margarine to cooked vegies.

- Remember: fruit with a little ice cream is better than no fruit at all!

Don't:

- Fuss, cajole or bribe children to eat vegetables.

- Despair if they keep saying 'no thanks'; exposure is all-important here.

- Sneer at frozen or tinned vegetables.

- Expect children to eat vegies that you find tasteless.

- Give up. Fruit and veg are important for children.

But there are some tricks and, like superannuation, a small, early, regular investment gives good long-term results. Exposure is the key. See the box on page 85 for suggestions.

Weight and losing weight

It seems seriously unfair that some people eat enormously yet remain thin, while others go plump on the thought of a chip. In the past, it was thought to be quite simple: overweight was caused by overeating. But now we realise that fatness or thinness is greatly determined by genetic predisposition, which is then modified by the type of food consumed and the energy that is expended.

A University of Sydney study has found that if a child is overweight at age eight, he has a fifty per cent chance of being overweight for the rest of his life.

The overweight baby or toddler will usually tone up and grow into an adult of normal size. But weight is much more serious at school-age, because the fat child tends to become a fat adult. The number of overweight and obese children is increasing (see box opposite). Who knows what heights will be reached at the next survey (2005).

	Overweight children	Obese children	Total
1985[1]	10%	1.3%	11.3%
1995[2]	15%	5%	20%

1. Australian Health and Fitness survey 1985
2. National Nutrition survey 1995

Adults find it relatively easy to maintain weight, but losing weight is many times more difficult. Fortunately, growing young children have an advantage: it is usually sufficient for them to maintain but not lose weight. So as an overweight child grows in height their steady weight will gradually slip into a body of perfect proportion.

Losing weight for any child or adult must be approached as a long-term project. It is achieved by changing the balance of food intake and increasing exercise. So while we can't change our genes, we can change diet and exercise. As weight increases, the ability to exercise reduces and that makes sensible food intake even more important.

Sensible food intake

Cut down on these	Try more of these
fatty meat, sausages, salami and other smallgoods	lean meat, chicken, fish (canned or fresh)
cakes, biscuits, snack foods (crisps, etc) pastries, croissants	bread, rolls, plain buns, plain crackers, pasta, rice
full-cream milk, yoghurt, cheese, cream and ice cream	skimmed or semi-skimmed milk, low-fat yoghurt, low-fat cheeses, low-fat ice cream, frozen yoghurt
fruit juices, fizzy drinks, sports drinks	fruit, vegetables, water, diluted fruit juices
fried foods	grilled or baked food with little fat
butter, margarine, oil	low-fat spreads or butter substitutes that are light on kcals

Exercise

As well as diet there must be an increase in exercise. Regular exercise keeps muscles strong, helps mental state and improves sleep. It controls weight and seems to lower the levels of the dangerous LDL cholesterol in the blood. The aim is to start them young and to develop patterns that we hope will last a lifetime.

With today's technology you don't even have to move a buttock to adjust the telly. As adults, we should try to walk instead of drive, use stairs instead of lifts and be more mobile in every part of our day. As for our children, we should walk with them to the shops, ride bikes and swim together. Television and computers should be limited and replaced with play. We should encourage them to play sport by being interested and supportive.

Limit commercial TV during children's viewing times. Almost four out of every five food ads are for 'junk' foods, so kids get bombarded with messages to eat foods that are not healthy. Powerful stuff. Recent research has shown that kids eat more junk after exposure to junk food ads, and overweight kids even more.

ELEVEN

Going Solo

It is estimated that between one-quarter and one-third of today's children will be living with just one parent at some time before they have left school. No matter

The main priority is always the emotional wellbeing of our children.

how positively we approach sole parenthood, it can make life immensely difficult. Even with the most amicable divorce settlement there is usually a major change to the stability and living standard of the family. This chapter is not about the rights of parents; it's about children who are being hurt and how we can protect their welfare.

The damage

Our young ones are damaged by a mix of hostility, instability, frequent moves, and people coming in and out of their life. We counter this by aiming for an amicable settlement and the minimum of change.

How children hurt

The under-sixes: will usually be quite open in their reaction, with an immediate and often intense response to the break. They don't know what it means but they

Common problems

- Unresolved hostility: ongoing anger, especially concerning access.

- Disruption and instability: move of home and school; move away from friends and local community.

- Lack of support: isolated from friends and extended family.

- Economic hardship: child poverty is commonly associated with sole parenthood; poverty affects the stability of housing and life.

- Unavailability: the parent may have to work unreasonable hours or is so stressed they are emotionally unavailable.

- New relationships: step situations cause difficulties, especially with older children.

dislike how it feels. However, children of this young age recover quickly once the adults get their act together.

The six- to eight-year-old: is in the middle ground where they almost, but don't quite, understand. They know this is a major event but may not realise that it is permanent.

Never underestimate the effect of stress on children. Parents may feel angry, but that's their problem, not the child's. Children of this age may worry that they are in some way responsible for the split. They also worry about being abandoned and replaced. Their reaction and the depth of their hurt still depends on the stability and emotional resilience of the caring parent.

The eight- to twelve-year-old: understands the implications of the split and understands it is forever. Often they will take sides and have confused loyalties. They may show bravado and a false disinterest, but behind this can be intense anger at what their parents have done. Most of their upset is open, but at this age they may bottle up emotions that can smoulder for years.

The adolescent: in the past it was thought that children of this age remained relatively unscathed by divorce but now it is believed they carry the greatest hurt. This is a point in life when children are fighting to make sense of their own personal relationships. Their confidence is shot when their role models screw up so spectacularly. Many worry that they may follow their parents' example.

How children react

There are three ways that a school-age child may react to major upset.

1. Clinging close

Clinging is most common in children under the age of six years. They don't understand our adult antics, but they feel they have been abandoned by 50 per cent of those they trust. Clingy children hold tight to the remaining parent. They shadow their mum around the house and they're reluctant to separate at the school gate for fear that Mum may not return at pick-up time. At night they procrastinate about bed and many insist on sleeping with their mother. The child's action makes good sense, but some parents are blind to what is happening.

2. Acting out

When a child feels stress they may transmit it back as bad behaviour. Younger children don't understand what is going on – they just react. Older children can be more vindictive and may single out one parent to abuse. Unfortunately, it is the parent who gives most love and care who usually gets the hardest kick.

Acting out is a particular problem when parents are emotionally fragile and intolerant of irritation. The child picks up on the stress in their home and reacts with irritating behaviour. The parent retaliates with anger, the child gets more distressed and their behaviour worsens. This starts a vicious circle, which, if not nipped in the bud, can escalate.

3. Taking it to heart

Though most children transmit their hurt outwards in the form of difficult behaviour, sometimes a once outgoing child appears distant, moody and lacking spark. School grades may slip, although occasionally a child may escape their unhappiness by overfocusing on study.

Some older children bottle up their feelings and withdraw.

Often they lose interest in friends and activities that used to give pleasure.

These children need to be able to talk about their feelings, but often their parents are so overwhelmed by their own problems they are emotionally unavailable when their children try to open up.

Protecting our children
Amicable access

Visits are going to happen whether we accept the inevitable or create trouble. If you are interested in your own, and your children's mental health, make access as peaceful as possible.

Arrange the times in advance so that everyone knows where they stand. Accept that things will not always be done as you would like, but with joint custody, you cannot make unrealistic demands.

Don't send the child with a list of petty conditions that dictate what they must wear, where they may go and who they may meet.

Unfortunately, even amicable access can confuse children. When Mum and Dad appear so civil the youngsters may wonder why their parents don't stop the nonsense and get back together. But civil it has to be.

Consistency and stability

When the adults in a child's life have lost the plot, the child maintains stability through consistent people and places. They do best when they still have their school,

Children need to know they will have two parents and both will continue to care for them. their friends, their extended family and the security of their own home.

Until the dust has settled, make no move or change that is not essential. Try to remain in the same district, at the same school and, if possible, in the same home. It is tempting to run away from unhappy memories but your home community provides the best base.

Don't divorce the grandparents

Little children are unsettled by the change in their parents' life, and they rely on relatives from both sides to provide a vital safety net.

You may divorce your partner, but your children do not want to divorce their grandparents. With break-ups children need the security of grandparents. If relatives are prepared to keep out of the politics and give support, they should have the most open of access. An amicable settlement involves being amicable to all friends and relatives who genuinely wish to help.

Starting a new relationship

After a split children can become extremely possessive of the parent who provides care. Often the sole parent and child develop an unusually close relationship, which will be fiercely guarded if someone tries to come between them. There is no trouble when Mum has a superficial friendship, but when a new companion competes for love and attention, children see this as a threat.

Younger children (under eight years) are generally reasonably accommodating. But older children are quite clear; they already have a dad and they don't need another. They also know they have been hurt once, and don't want a second dose. Teenagers are usually obtuse in the extreme.

Success comes with slow steps and gaining confidence over time.

PART TWO

TWELVE

Troubleshooting:
Behaviours A–Z

Here are some of the most common behaviour problems and how to tackle them. What you will use will depend on only one thing – getting the right result.

If you would like more information after reading this section, please move on to *Beyond Toddlerdom*.

Contents

Nightmares	Sleep walking
Night terrors	Socially out of tune
Obsessive behaviour	Soiling, or encopresis
Only children	Stealing
Oppositional	Suicide talk
behaviour	Suspension from school
Organisation	Television, computers and
Pocket money	the Internet
Pretend friends	Thumb sucking
School refusal	Tidying the bedroom
Sex	Tooth grinding
Short fuse	Whingeing
Shyness	Zzz: sleep problems

Accident prone

Some children are an accident waiting to happen. So how can we help the impulsive child who shoots from the hip? Child safety must always be the first priority. Teach the traffic light technique of 'Stop. Think. Go'. (Slow the pace, then encourage them to reflect for a moment, then act.) It sounds very simple but it is a challenge when children are all go and no stop.

Accident proneness is a classic symptom of Attention

Deficit Hyperactivity Disorder (ADHD). Please refer to *The Pocket Guide to Understanding ADHD* for more detail. If the child is found to be suffering from ADHD and is successfully treated, they will be much safer.

Arguing and backchat

Children argue in order to hijack attention, look smart or push a power struggle. Here are some ways to handle a keen arguer:

> **Keep asking yourself, 'Is this getting me anywhere?'**

■ If possible, ask, don't tell.

■ Be enthusiastic, show interest, be positive.

■ Change tack with a different intonation or a whisper.

■ Use an 'I' statement: 'I feel sad when we argue'.

■ Give feedback for good times: 'Gosh, you are such good company'.

Bad language

In the early school years children use a lot of silly language like 'poo' and 'bum'. There's no malice; it's just part of the fun and nonsense of being young. At this age children repeat words they have heard at school, but they have no knowledge of their meaning. Words may also be used to wind up Mum and Dad.

For the under-six, even the word 'bottom' can be as entertaining as an entire season of 'Seinfeld'.

By late primary school, bad language is normal behaviour for the herd. At this age it is important to make it clear what we will and will not accept.

Here are a number of approaches, but what you use will depend on the age of the child, the extent of the problem and the reason for the bad language.

- When language is used to bait parents, where possible, let it pass.

- Allow the use of almost rude words: 'Shoot!' or 'Fruit cake!'

  In young children explain the silliness of describing reproductive anatomy in public.

- Put limits on swearing. 'You can use those words, but not here'.

- Give a warning and follow with time out.

- Finally, set a good example: children parrot the

speech, abusive attitudes and bad language of those they are close to.

Bed wetting

At the age of five years, ten per cent of children will still wet the bed. Bed wetting (nocturnal enuresis) is due to a late maturation in normal bladder function. It is not in any way deliberate or of emotional origin. The treatment of bed wetting involves the following:

■ A waterproof mattress cover.

■ Lift last thing at night. They go to sleep at 8pm, then at 11pm they are brought to the toilet.

■ The most effective treatment for bed wetting is a pad-and-bell alarm (hire from children's hospitals, some community health centres and chemists). A small sensor is attached to the pants or placed below the bottom sheet. When the flood arrives the sensor shorts out, sets off a buzzer and you have red alert. The child has to be motivated, and they must be

Emotional upset does not cause chronic enuresis but chronic enuresis can cause emotional upset.

completely awake during clean up. The alarm should stay in place until the child has stayed dry every night for a reasonable period.

■ If the pad-and-bell doesn't work, your GP can prescribe a short-acting preparation that can help your child stay dry through the night.

Bike riding

Bikes can give children a great release for pent-up energy as well as freedom and mobility. We usually remove trainer wheels when the child is about five years old, but children continue to need close supervision until eight or nine years. It's important to have rules in place right from the start.

■ Have clear rules about helmets, stopping at inter-sections, crossing main roads and areas that are off limits.

Bike ride as a family. This is good for children and helps unfit adults avoid heart attacks.

■ Have rules about care of the bike, locking and putting it away at night.

■ Supervise when children are challenging their friends on jumps, ramps and riding through the air.

■ When rules are disregarded, lock up the bicycle for a week and don't debate or argue your actions.

Birthday parties

Younger children are full of bubble and bounce. Parents tell me that sugar in the party food is the cause of this over-the-top behaviour. I'm not so sure: this age group would be airborne even if we fed them on the purest of sugar-free food and natural spring water.

■ Check all toilets are capable of quick throughput and full flush!

■ For timid partygoers, talk it through before they go. Role-play introductions and 'thankyous'.

A trick candle (that won't blow out) on the birthday cake never fails to impress.

■ With an over-rowdy raver, arrive a little late and pick up a little early.

■ When organising your own child's party, ensure you have enough adult minders on hand.

■ Consider using an outside party centre. It may not be more expensive and it has the advantage that others tidy up.

Bragging and boasting

The under-sevens live in a world where everything is larger and more spectacular than life. How you handle a boast depends on the child's age, the extent of the problem and the state of their esteem.

- For minor bragging, ignore it altogether.

- Explain how boasting can make you look stupid.

- With tall stories, listen and then state, 'I hear what you are saying but this is not quite true.'

- Notice non-bragging days or weeks. 'Today you played a blinder of a game, you were brilliant, yet not a brag or a boast!'

- Don't be too tough. Life would be pretty boring if we didn't stretch the realms of credibility.

Every successful author knows that you can't let truth get in the way of a good story.

Breaks in unthinking rage

When children have a short fuse they may overreact and even destroy their own treasures. After the event they see the stupidity of their behaviour, which makes them twice as stroppy.

The angriest human beings are those who are angry at their own silliness.

- Don't nag or say, 'Told you so', as this adds insult to injury.

- If they break something important to them – for example, an almost-completed model aeroplane – support, don't criticise.

- Don't rub salt in the wound. Even if they say they don't care, they hurt deeply.

Breaks their sibling's property

Some children have fiddly fingers. They have to touch and things get broken. Here's what you can do:

- Have a small number of rules about what can and what cannot be touched.

- Notice when care and respect is shown for other people's property.

- Distinguish between the occasional unthinking act and damage that follows the deliberate disregard of a warning.

- Instruct siblings to keep their treasures secure and make their personal space a no-go area.

- Breakages can be replaced via a small levy on the pocket money.

- Don't set up an impossibly harsh repayment system as this causes resentment and hostility.

Bullies and teasing

Children only bully because they have low self-esteem and feel uplifted by dragging others down. Some have poor social skills and are overly slow to realise they have overstepped the mark.

Our aim is to teach our children to fight with their brains rather than with their bodies.

Bullies target the impulsive, short-fused child because they provide a jackpot every time.

- When a **five- or six-year-old** is victimised, parents should discuss the problem with the school teacher or principal. They can deal with the problem through extra supervision, general class instruction about the treatment of fellow humans, or attach a buddy for extra support.

■ When children are **eight or older** parents can discuss the problem discreetly. Use role-play at home to show how to sidestep conflict, such as getting them to count quietly to five, walk away or teach them to develop assertiveness by using words: 'That's my property'; 'I'm not going to chase you'.

Car travel

Just because adults like long-distance driving, it doesn't necessarily follow that this suits their children. If your child fights, squabbles and protests on the trip to the corner store, a 500-kilometre car trip could be a challenge. In case you have to take that trip, though, here are some ideas:

■ Before you start, set down the ground rules about teasing, poking and annoying.

■ Plan regular breaks and keep the passengers informed of the time to touchdown.

■ If the car tape player is to be used for everybody, allocate tape time in advance.

■ A Walkman may help.

■ Construct a token system where short periods of peaceful travel are rewarded with a small token (a tick, star, bead, etc.). These all add up to a worthwhile reward (such as spending money) at the next fuel stop.

Try securing a large piece of luggage between the occupants of the back seat.

Chores

It is important to introduce chores at a young age, as this capitalises on the under-fives' wish to be helpful. Give a few responsibilities, then build on this with age. Here's what to do:

■ Clearly communicate what you expect from your children.

■ Work together where possible, as this gets jobs done and helps relationships.

■ Give one reminder, but don't nag.

The ultimate aim is to encourage children to see what needs to be done and get on with it without being asked . . . if only!

- Appreciate effort, and notice when tasks are done without asking.

- Pay a basic level of pocket money then add a bonus for work completed without complaint.

Clinginess

One- and two-year-olds are clingy by nature but this eases with age, and most will separate confidently by three or four. However, there are a few who still cling right into the early school years.

- Steer gently and go with the flow. Little people vary in their ability to separate and they have another seventy-five years to sort things out.

- Let them know about visitors before they arrive. Role-play eye contact, greetings and small talk.

- Don't push. They know how they feel and don't need railroading by some insensitive adult.

- When reacting to family change, tread softly. They need all their supports at this time.

Conflict cycle

This negative spiral is one of the most damaging situations. The parent gets angry, the child returns fire, no one backs down and resentment builds. But this is not a holy war: forget about who is right or wrong. Without compromise and change everyone will end up in the wrong.

Whatever the cause, the only remedy is to get in early, then teach parents to use an olive branch rather than a stick.

- Avoid cold, condescending tones, quiet anger and passive aggression.

- Be positive and transmit the message that you expect action.

- Avoid 'you' statements like 'You expect everything'. Instead, use 'I' statements: 'I feel sad that we annoy each other this way'.

- Notice and appreciate any small gesture of compliance and closeness.

- Have a round-table conference. Discuss how you annoy each other. Each side can then try to change two specific behaviours. Review progress one week later.

Dawdling and won't get dressed

I am told there are children who jump with enthusiasm out of bed, get dressed and are ready for school hours ahead of time. But this endangered species is outnumbered by whole divisions of dawdlers. These come in two sorts: those created with a dreamy, slow-moving brain, and the ones who go slow to damage their parents' health.

The dreamy starter:

■ Needs to be woken early and reminded many times. It's good practice to make sure their clothes are laid out and ready the night before, and to reward them for the little steps they make. The secret is to nudge gently yet be immensely patient.

The deliberate dawdler:

■ Also needs an early start, but after this, only allow a limited number of reminders. After two or three prompts, set the kitchen timer to announce ten minutes before departure. If the child is running late, that's their problem and they must sort this out with the school.

Daydreaming

Some children are created with a dreamy temperament. Teachers despair as the child glazes over and their thoughts slip out the window.

Other children switch off to escape from the difficulties in their life. We often see this with family breakdowns and other unhappiness. If a previously sparky, alert child becomes detached and uninterested, suspect an emotional trigger or even depression.

Sometimes we can't change the daydreamer; we can only change our expectations.

After the age of eleven years children develop the ability to use abstract thinking. Some of these older children become dreamers as the potential Einstein tries to think through a new theory of relativity.

Here are some tips for dealing with dreamers:

■ Dreamers need structure, encouragement and reminders of time.

■ Work beside the child to keep the focus on the task at hand. Use a kitchen timer to add some urgency to homework completion or eating dinner.

Death

How a child responds to death will depend on how close they were to the person who died and how their life is disrupted. Also, a child's reaction to death varies greatly with age.

- The under-six-year-old has no grasp of the finality of death.

- The six- to eight-year-old may have hidden worries, which can be made worse if parents don't keep them informed.

- The eight- to twelve-year-old is developing an understanding of death and needs to be allowed to grieve.

Depression

Depression is more than the kind of short-term sadness we all experience. True depression immobilises, dulls interest and turns out the light at the end of the tunnel.

Though our greatest worry is the depressed teenager, children of all ages can be depressed.

The depressed five-year-old becomes unhappy, quiet and less animated, usually in response to an upsetting life event. Depression in a ten-year-old may be less obvious. The main symptom is a change in their usual outgoing state.

Be alert to a change such as the child withdrawing from friends and interests.

■ The child's feelings are real. It's pointless to suggest they pull themselves together. They would do this if they could.

■ Try to keep the child busy. Encourage them to get up at weekends, get out and look neat.

■ Encourage them to talk about, write down or draw how they feel.

■ Try to distinguish the common martyr statements like 'I'm ugly' or 'No one would care if I die' from a true call for help.

■ A child with severe learning problems is vulnerable to depression. It is hard to show them the achievement they so much need.

■ Professional psychological or psychiatric help is recommended for all depressed children. Drugs like Zoloft and Prozac may bring some gains. Help is a matter of urgency when self-harm is a possibility.

■ Encourage outside interests and looking forward to something.

Diet and behaviour

In about 5 per cent of all children diet affects their behaviour, and their most common symptom is irritability or restlessness.

In my experience, when there is a sensitivity, parents are usually aware of the offending drink, food or fruit and give this a miss.

There are four common groups of chemicals that cause food intolerance:

■ The salicylates are natural chemicals found in many fruits, vegetables, nuts, herbs, spices and jams; highest in unripe fruits.

■ The amines occur in high levels in cheese, chocolate, yeast extract and fruits such as bananas (especially when overripe).

■ Monosodium glutamate (MSG) occurs naturally in strong flavoured foods like tomatoes and cheeses and is also sometimes used as an additive in stock cubes, yeast extracts and some styles of cooking.

■ Food additives: for example, sulphites are numbered between 220 and 228, while antioxidants are numbered 310 to 321.

■ Sugar is the target of much criticism but this has not been shown to cause behavioural problems. I rarely suggest the diet approach to behaviour, but I support parents who want to give it a fair go. For them I recommend that the diet be supervised by a knowledgeable dietitian.

But diet has a lesser effect on behaviour than popular belief might suggest.

Fears

Children have different worries at different ages. A three-year-old might be terrified of loud noises, electric hand dryers, ambulance sirens and dogs. By six years they may fear the dark, falling, losing their mum, wind, thunder, ghosts and monsters. At ten years they worry about school failure, speaking in front of the class, looking foolish, how they appear and possible friction in their parents' marriage.

■ Most school-age fears are fed into our children by what they see in the world or hear from their parents. Our necessary warnings about road safety, stranger danger and home security may cause our children to fear injury, abduction and burglars.

■ Miscommunication also raises fears. When Grandma is rushed to hospital it is often easier to say she has a severe cold than explain heart failure. But if Grandma dies in hospital, the child's next cold may be seen as a serious event.

Forgetfulness

With the disorganised and forgetful you can't work miracles, but memory jogs help reliability.

■ Write notes and 'To do' lists.

■ Write a reminder word on their hand.

■ Put a rubber band on one wrist to remind them.

■ Wear the watch on the wrong wrist to jog their memory.

Many children have been created with all the forgetfulness of an absent-minded professor and need all the memory jogs we can give.

■ Have a chart on the fridge door that lists all important activities throughout the week, and encourage them to refer to it regularly.

Gratitude

'It's not fair,' Dad unloads to me. 'I took him to the zoo, we had a fantastic day of father–son togetherness then, on leaving, he saw a Mr Whippy van, created a scene and grizzled all the way home. I bust myself for him – so where's the gratitude?'

I have news for you. Don't expect gratitude in this world. Your reward will come in the hereafter! You are in this parenting because you love them, not for thanks and reward.

Enjoy it when you receive gratitutde from your children – even if it's a once-a-year event.

Many children are full of thanks and appreciation, but for others it's all take and no give. If it makes you feel better, deliver them a lecture about the injustice of it all, but it won't change anything.

Grazing

There are some children who nibble all day like sheep. Grazing is not unhealthy as long as the pasture is of reasonable quality.

For some, grazing is their favourite way to feed. Others graze out of restless boredom. In school holidays these are the children who pace around, opening and closing doors until the fridge is unable to keep food cool.

■ The solution to boredom is to steer children towards more structured activity.

■ When scavengers are on the prowl lock away the goodies and avoid buying treat snacks.

■ Bored or not, grazers need easy access to healthy affordable snacks. A chilled jug of tap water, unflavoured milk (preferably low fat), bread, fruit and plain biscuits are a start.

Hair and eyebrow plucking

I have seen school-age children with no eyebrows or eyelashes and others with thin hair or even a patch of baldness.

If there is some obvious cause of tension this must be addressed, otherwise adopt the gentle redirection, minimum-fuss approach.

■ Children usually pull and chew when they are bored, falling asleep or watching television.

■ Consider getting something more appropriate to twiddle, like a worry ball.

- Give a gentle nudge but don't ridicule them as this increases the tension and they will become an underground plucker.

- Have fancy hairstyles and focus on attractive eyebrows and lashes. Be quick to notice any improvement or any area of regeneration.

The pleasure children get from pulling out and nibbling their hair is probably similar to what they get out of nail biting and finger picking.

Homework hassles

Most children see homework as a necessary evil that has to be done, but for some it's about procrastination, foot dragging and excuses. In the early years homework plays a small part in learning but by teenage the ability to organise, stick at a task and study independently is vital for tertiary success. The ways to encourage homework are:

- Have knowledge and interest in the syllabus, check that work is completed and be enthusiastic about marks for effort.

- Have a regular homework time and keep strictly to this every day.

Establish the importance of home study right from the start.

- ■ Work in a special place that is always associated with homework.

- ■ If attention span is weak, expect twenty minutes full output, a ten-minute break, then twenty minutes more. Use a timer to act as a referee.

- ■ Some children manage better when homework is done before arrival home. Some children are morning people. Not everyone is the same.

- ■ Don't let homework destroy your parent–child relationship. If it gets too heated, discuss the options with the class teacher.

Interrupting

Children who are impulsive or forgetful may interrupt. The impulsive have no patience and can't wait. The forgetful will lose their words if they don't get them out immediately. We want to keep the lines of communication open but also encourage them to wait.

- ■ Give a gentle reminder: 'Your turn in a minute, John'.

- Keep repeating the rules of conversation, without becoming a nag.

- Allow the forgetful child to interrupt with a cue word that you pick up later. As you are talking they say 'New teacher,' and when appropriate you ask, 'What's this about a new teacher?'

- Teach through role-play how to interpret body language. Show when you are receptive and when your eyes are telling them to back off.

Lying and bending the truth

Children under the age of eight years tend to be open with their parents and are quite transparent in their dishonesty. But by ten years their deceit is much more subtle and some events in their lives are guarded with secrecy.

Before the age of eight children are immensely open. If we encourage this when they are young, they will confide more in their tempestuous teens.

- With the four- to six-year-old, don't overreact. Calmly say, 'I don't think this is true'.

129

- Make sure that honesty pays off. There must be less punishment for owning up than denying fault.

- Notice their honesty and appreciate their openness.

Martyrdom

Martyrdom is still alive and well and being practised by many six- to twelve-year-olds. They approach their Mum, look pathetic and state, 'I'm dumb. I'm ugly. You don't love me. I've got no friends.' Occasionally some of this may be true, but for most, martyrdom is used to get an avalanche of attention.

Through the ages, martyrs have shown great talent at grabbing attention. It may seem a bit extreme to be stoned or burned but it sure puts you on centre stage.

We don't want to be insensitive to genuine concerns but when playing for attention, remember:

- Martyrs get nowhere without an audience.

- Avoid getting dragged into debates about intellect, good looks and their number of friends.

- Make a brief statement: 'You are clever and brilliant at

swimming'; 'I think you are a real good looker'. Then give a reassuring cuddle and move on.

Meal-time behaviour

Every night the evening meal provides time when families can sit, listen and relate.

■ Turn a relatively blind eye to mess and imperfect manners.

■ Don't let squabbles and nitpicking cause stress. We want peace, not perfection. **It is essential that the television is switched off.**

■ Establish basic rules about leaving the table, rushing and dawdling.

■ Rushers must stay for a certain time and when they depart, they should leave the room.

■ Dawdlers are given time, then left to sit by themselves. If dawdling is extreme, set a cooking timer and when it rings, clear the table.

■ Give feedback for good manners.

Nail biting and finger picking

Nail biting probably occurs in about one in three eight-year-olds, one in two fifteen-year-olds and one in four at the age of twenty.

Biting is worse when tense, bored or watching television. Whatever happens, don't nag, nitpick and create a battle.

- Keep better occupied during peak biting times.

- Compare their nails against other unbitten nails.

- When enough nail appears, manicure and make this special.

- Prepare a star chart to focus on each two hours without a pick or bite.

- Consider your chemist's best anti-bite nail paint. This may tip the balance but only when there is motivation.

Nightmares

A nightmare is an unsettling dream that leaves a child upset and semi-awake. They respond to our comfort, drift back to sleep and are aware of what happened the next day. Children have their most disturbed dreams when sick.

Creative parents use ghost repellent spray. This is a simple water spray with glitter particles in the bottom. Spray around doors and windows for guaranteed security.

- Come to the child, hold, stroke, comfort, soothe.

- Turn over the pillow. The cool side has special properties that prevent bad dreams!

- Place a dim light in the room.

- Talk about dreams by day to emphasise what is real and what is pretend.

- Allow frightened children to come to your bed.

Night terrors

Night terrors are different from nightmares. They are not a dream, just an uncomfortable move through the deepest part of sleep. The child cries out apparently frightened, yet totally switched off, open-eyed and unaware. In the morning they have no recollection of any disturbance.

Night terrors are more common in the preschool and younger school ages.

■ Nothing seems to soothe; all we can do is to stay close, talk gently and wait until they settle.

■ They occur in the early part of the night and, if regular, can be avoided by waking the child half an hour before the usual time of terror.

Obsessive behaviour

There are thousands of children out there who are normal yet very unusual. Most are boys and most have a preoccupation with order, routine and an area of over-interest. They may have an immense knowledge of animals, cars, planes, football, video titles or events in history.

One eight-year-old I worked with had an obsessive bath routine. Only he could insert the plug, and the bath water could only rise to a certain level. The bath couldn't end until he had lifted out his toys and placed them in an exact spot. Then he removed the plug and some normality returned.

- Many of these children are fixated on some part of learning.

- Sometimes there is a worrying overinterest in wars, guns and death.

At school some are branded 'weird', while others are accepted as an eccentric professor.

- Their conversation is often inappropriate, turning into a lecture on their special topic.

- As I work with these children I must decide when this is a normal odd temperament and when it is a pathological problem such as Asperger syndrome or autism spectrum disorder.

- When in any doubt, children who may have obsessive behaviour should be referred to a paediatrician, child psychiatrist or specialist in child development.

Only children

The only child is often said to be lonely, spoiled and over-influenced by adults. There is a seed of truth in this, but there is more to the story. On average, the only

There is a saying, 'It takes a village to raise a child'. I think a village full of people is more important than a brother or sister in an empty city.

child gets more stimulation, education and individual attention at home.

■ This shows as a slight increase in academic ability, and they are more in tune with adult thinking.

■ I believe that an extended family upbringing is of more importance than having a brother or sister. This lets children see their roots and gives them experience with babies and family relationships as well as a respect for the elders of the tribe.

Oppositional behaviour

One of the most common and difficult problems I see is

Parents with compliant children have no understanding of how difficult this can be.

the child with entrenched opposition. When this problem is in its most minor form the child is reluctant to comply with any request. Major opposition generates immense hostility, which ruins relationships.

There is good and bad news about opposition. The bad is the damage it does to families where mums and dads may get no pleasure from parenting. The **Don't rely on reason. This does not impress the oppositional child.**

good news is that most turn into well-adjusted, normal adults. Many will later feel remorse and wish they had done things differently.

- Opposition is extremely hard to treat. Be realistic in your expectations. A twenty per cent change in six months is an appropriate goal.

- Go gently with the difficult three- and four-year-old. This is the best age to nip opposition in the bud. Be positive, encourage the good, let the unimportant pass and steer around confrontation.

- With the oppositional school-age child avoid debate, as this escalates and places parents on the back foot.

- Avoid hostile, cold, passive-aggressive or sarcastic comments.

- Avoid ultimatums and rigid limits. These provide a clear line to challenge.

- Avoid backing the child into a corner. Allow them to

feel they have some choice and power over the outcome: 'You can choose not to do your homework now but you will be choosing not to watch "The Simpsons". It's your choice.'

Immediately grasp any good behaviour and appreciate the positives.

- Talk in a calm, matter-of-fact way. Use the broken record technique, quietly repeating the message.

- Use the technique of active ignoring. Briefly move to another room, or water the garden, then return and re-engage.

- Use an 'I' statement: 'I feel sad when we are angry with each other'.

- Make your statement and move on. Don't hang around waiting for retaliation.

Organisation

I don't know when a person first has that ability to stop, think ahead and then move on. I doubt if there is much planning before the age of eight years, and in some humans, organisation is never a strong suit.

■ At school age our goal is to get children to stop, think and plan. We can help this by asking at bedtime, 'What do you need to bring to school? Any sport or swimming?'

Some parents act like the entertainment officer on a cruise ship: each morning they post the day's program on the fridge door.

■ Before leaving for school ask them to stop for a minute and run through the checklist.

■ As children get older we should encourage notes and 'To do' lists, and we direct the focus onto priorities.

■ As exam success is so essential we need to teach children to be organised in tests: 'Read the question carefully. Stick to the instructions. There are six questions and there's one hour. That's ten minutes for each question.'

Pocket money

Little children have no need for pocket money before they start school. A six-year-old gets a small allowance that is usually squandered or lent to their older sister,

By teenage years it takes crisp notes, gold bars or share-option certificates to have an effect. the con-artist. But by the age of eight years the potential Bonds and Bransons have realised that money talks. These short-pants entrepreneurs can be motivated by the sight of a silver coin.

The amount of pocket money depends on how much you can afford, what extras the child must buy and your neighbourhood norm. After this you have two choices:

1. Pay a fixed weekly sum that is reviewed each year, with adjustments based on inflation, the world economy and how you are feeling on that day.

2. Provide a base salary, then pay double for each day that work is completed without reminders or complaint.

Pretend friends

At my age, if I start talking to imaginary people you would probably call for a straitjacket. But normal young children are allowed to talk and play with pretend people.

If your child prattles on to some pretend person, just relax and enjoy this brief window of undisturbed innocence.

■ This occurs in about one in ten children, usually starting at about the age of three years, an age of technicolour imagination.

One little boy used to bring a dinosaur on a rope when he visited me in my office.

■ The friend is usually of the same sex as the child and always has a name.

■ The child is actually quite aware of what is fact and fiction. Imaginary friends are not a sign of disturbance, loneliness or emotional stress.

■ They are more common in girls and may signify a more creative style of temperament.

■ These friends have usually evaporated by the age of six years.

School refusal

It is quite common for a child to start school with great enthusiasm then, after several weeks, have a change of heart. The child has a point: if we make home life so good, why should they want to go to school?

At older ages, school refusal is a more serious problem. Sometimes it is due to learning difficulty or the child is

Absence makes them see home as a pretty special place and they decide to opt for early graduation.

socially uncomfortable. If you see it from their point of view, why should they go to a place that causes such pain?

■ The first step in managing school refusal is to return the child to the classroom. Missing school is like falling off a horse: if you don't get in the saddle now it becomes much more difficult in the future.

■ If decisive returns and quick exits have not worked, the parents and class teacher need to meet and work out a joint plan. Dad will drive the child to school and walk in the gate with them, but then they are in the hands of the class teacher and they must stay.

■ When the situation is stuck in deadlock the school counsellor will provide more specialised support.

Sometimes it is a parent who secretly clings to their child and generates separation anxiety.

■ School refusal can be a psychological symptom such as where a child is frightened to leave their mum or dad.

142

Sex

Children are created in two sorts: little girls and little boys. At the age of six years, their size and physical strength are very similar. Then, somewhere between the age of ten and fourteen years, the pubertal growth spurt will start. Girls are first to take off, and for a brief time are taller and more physically strong than the male of the species. After this there are considerable differences between the sexes, the male becoming larger and stronger, the female probably more mature and sensible.

Though adolescence is the age that causes most sexual concern for parents, the attitudes to sex that are important are laid down very much earlier.

I. Sex education

- Start early.
- Answer genuine questions clearly and simply.

2. Sexual development

- Girls reach puberty between ten and thirteen years.
- Boys reach puberty between ten and a half and fifteen years.

■ How early or late a child develops may follow a family pattern.

■ If you have any concerns about your child's sexual development, talk to your paediatrician.

3. Other sex-related issues

Sexual abuse is most often committed by a known and trusted adult or adolescent. This is more likely than we are prepared to admit.

■ Masturbation is normal, healthy and usually innocent in children.

■ Homosexuality is probably part of an individual's biological make-up.

■ Cross-dressing in children is not unusual and should be managed with minimum fuss, unless the child overstates it or is persistent for a year or more, in which case, see your paediatrician.

■ Families who are open in communication and free from sexual hang-ups produce children who develop the most appropriate adult attitudes.

Short fuse

The smallest unimportant event can trigger the most unexpected explosion in these children. At school the sparky child is sought out by bullies who know they are easy to stir. When upset they may go berserk and hit out, and many may be suspended from school.

There are a lot of sparky children, some with the stability of out-of-date gelignite.

Poor impulse control is predominantly a boy problem, though girls, including mothers, are not exempt. This style of temperament has a strong hereditary link, and many of these children are like a parent or grandparent.

Mums and dads are in a dilemma about whether to stand firm and treat the child the same way they treat their other children or to back off and preserve the peace. The more I work with these children, the more often I promote the path of peace.

- With young children anticipate, avoid triggers, divert, keep calm.

- Avoid debate and argument; this inflames and escalates.

■ Put the child (or yourself!) in time out.

■ Do not interpret the hysterical actions of a child as premeditated or malicious.

■ With older children talk about the behaviour when they are calm. Get them to realise how stupid they appear in front of their friends.

One mum said, 'We get on much better if I avoid the word "no".' There are better ways to say it without using that word.

■ Try the 'traffic light' technique: stop, think and then go.

■ When impulsivity is part of ADHD, its treatment will dramatically improve this behaviour. See *The Pocket Guide to Understanding ADHD* for more detail.

Shyness

The world is divided into two types of people: extroverts and introverts. But there are very few true extroverts – just introverts pretending they are extroverts.

We should respect our child's temperament and not

try to change it. Shy children do not need to be belittled, forced or hassled. For them socialisation comes gradually with time.

So there are ways we can help our children at home when they are ready:

- Ask a friend home.

- Find other children with a common interest: computer addicts, sports clubs.

- Encourage conversation openers such as asking questions, making pleasantries.

- Teach them to read people: a welcoming smile, enthusiastic eyes, body movement!

Sleep walking

This is not a rare condition – about ten per cent of all children have an occasional walk and two per cent are quite regular. It's more common in boys and usually occurs in the early part of the night.

Sleep walking is not a dream state – these children are in the deepest part of sleep. They sit up and start to move in a stiff, robotic manner. Their eyes are glazed, yet they can navigate around obstacles, open doors and perform simple tasks. If addressed, they respond but the words are like computer speech or unintelligible. If woken, they are unaware, and in the morning they remember nothing. Each walk lasts a few minutes, though some can continue for up to an hour.

■ There is no need to wake the sleepwalker. This can be extremely difficult and causes nothing but confusion.

■ Bring them back to bed and protect them from danger.

■ Sleep walking lessens with age, though some are still on the move as adolescents or adults.

Socially out of tune

Most children are out and out charmers, but a few are socially clumsy. They play poorly, mix with difficulty and don't see how their behaviour irritates others. If you feel that your child may be socially out of tune there are some things you can do to help:

■ Reinforce when they play well and interact appropriately.

- Give a brief reminder when their actions are upsetting others.

- Don't become negative or constantly criticise.

- Discreetly ask them how it would feel if they were in the other person's place.

- Social skills training programs are sometimes suggested but these are often more successful in the therapy room than the outside world.

- The development of social skills comes gradually with age and maturity.

Soiling, or encopresis

I believe these children are created with a soil-prone gut, which is tipped over the edge by some trigger. This may result from the pain of constipation, the birth of a sibling, admission to hospital or stress in the family. But most commonly there is no obvious triggering event.

Almost two out of every 100 children at the age of seven years will still poo in their pants.

Some parents believe the child has control and the problem is deliberate. But this is not true: the children I see would like nothing better than to stop soiling. Often it takes an outside force to change entrenched human behaviour, such as a psychologist or paediatrician.

■ The first step in treatment is to exclude constipation. This is not always straightforward as some children are badly blocked yet present with the confusing symptom of diarrhoea.

■ Then encourage good behaviour with a simple star chart.

■ Begin by focusing on sitting three times a day: before school, following school and following dinner to encourage one moment of success.

■ Then we concentrate on regular usage and clean days.

■ About one-third respond to this rapidly, one-third take six months or more and the remainder are extremely hard to shift.

Stealing

Petty shoplifting or stealing is probably more common

than any parent wishes to acknowledge. It's tough, but unless the child faces up to their actions no lesson is learnt.

■ Goods must be returned and if this is not possible, repayment comes from future pocket money.

■ If possible, parents and child must front up to the shop.

■ If stealing ever becomes a major problem, you may need to seek help from a psychologist or community clinic.

Suicide talk

Youth suicide is a great concern and any child who talks of self-harm must be taken seriously. Though teens and young adults are at greatest risk, the child of ten years or younger can occasionally suicide.

■ Children will often say, 'I'm dumb. I'm bad. I've got no friends. What's the point in living? What would you do if I killed myself?'

Children are also at greater risk following the suicide of some major public figure or someone in their close community.

Nothing in this world is completely certain, so when in the slightest doubt be quick to ask for help.

■ The dilemma for parents is to separate these martyr statements from a genuine cry for help.

■ Though cautious, I generally underplay such comments in these younger ages, but only if all else is on track.

■ The alarm bells ring when there is a change in personality, loss of interest, withdrawal from friends, major sadness or an overfocus on the means of self-injury.

■ At this young age most of the talk of self-harm has the sole purpose of stirring up mums and dads.

Suspension from school

Most suspensions follow unthinking outbursts where a child hits, hurts, insults or gets so angry they refuse to comply.

■ With many school suspensions the wrong person has been blamed.

- When a child is suspended from school, always look past the reported crime to see why it happened. It may not change the decision, but the true culprits should be brought to justice.

  In my experience most of these children are kind, sensitive kids with no malice in their make-up. But when pushed too far they snap and hit trouble.

- When suspension results from the impulsivity of ADHD, this is the priority for treatment. See *The Pocket Guide to Understanding ADHD* for more detail.

- Parents will be annoyed but they must not get too heavy and bully the school. Even in suspension the parent–teacher relationship must be guarded at all costs.

Television, computers and the Internet

When they are used appropriately these can bring valuable skills and knowledge, but when they are misused, they can promote isolation, poor socialisation and glazed-eyed solitude.

1. Television

The most important goal is to switch from constant bombardment to the watching of specific programs.

Television channels beam a signal; parents control the power supply.

- When a chosen program is finished, turn off the set.

- Restrict viewing to one hour per day, with an absolute maximum of two hours per day.

- Recognise the effect of excessive television viewing on fitness and obesity.

- Don't watch television during family meals. Reintroduce talk and relating.

- Many studies have shown a direct link between violence on television and aggression in children and adults.

- Discuss the content of programs to provide a reality check.

- Limit news watching by both adults and children.

2. Computers

■ Agree on limits of use in advance.

■ Supervision is the key.

■ Start children off with fun educational software.

■ Avoid exposing your child to adult or violent games.

■ Games can develop your child's learning and motor skills.

3. The Internet

■ Agree on limits of use in advance.

■ Supervise children's access to the Internet.

■ The Internet can be educational, but teach children that not everything on the Net is 'true'.

■ Invest in an Internet screening program.

■ Teach children that personal information must not be given out.

Thumb sucking

This is an innocent habit, not a sign of emotional insecurity. It gives pleasure to one-third of young

A little gentle comfort is never a problem, but hours of heavy tooth bending could prove expensive.

children; the other two-thirds never suck their thumbs. The average age that children stop is three and a half years, though many continue until they're five and two per cent are still sucking at thirteen years.

Dentists become worried once the second teeth are about to appear, because heavy sucking increases the risk of protruding front teeth.

- At school age most thumb sucking is in times of boredom, tiredness and especially when settling to sleep.

- Never nag or become too heavy as this causes stress, which increases sucking and then drives it underground.

- When in doubt, talk to your dentist. They will advise and tell you if damage is occurring.

Tidying the bedroom

I often wonder if there is a tidiness gene. If there is, some children are born with this vital bit missing. The secret of tidiness is to start early. Children between the age of one and four years like to be helpful, so build on this while it is there. After the age of five there are a selection of suggestions:

Don't expect children to be more organised and tidy than their parents.

- Sort through toys, removing stuff that doesn't work and small items that constipate the vacuum cleaner.

- Before complaining, make sure your children know what you expect of them.

- Use a kitchen timer to count down to inspection.

- Use the 'carrot' incentive: 'You tidy this, I'll get your drink ready.'

- Be quick to notice effort and tidiness: 'Gosh, have the cleaners been here?'

- After giving adequate warning, place all untidied items in a large polythene bag. Lock this away for several days.

If you don't have this sorted out by teenage, take a step back and ask, 'Is it worth driving my children from home for the sake of a clean bedroom?'

Tooth grinding

Tooth grinding at night is extremely common in normal, well-adjusted children. Dentists worry that the repeated grinding can cause long-term tooth damage, while parents are more concerned by the noise.

■ Some people believe that tooth grinding can cause malocclusion of the jaw, while others suggest that malocclusion can be the reason why they grind.

■ Whatever is going on, discuss it with your dentist. If your child's teeth are becoming worn your dentist will provide a small night splint to give protection.

■ In your great grandmother's day tooth grinding was a sure sign of worm infestation. But she got her ends mixed up: any worm that is out and about at night is at the bottom, not the top end.

Whingeing

There is a remarkable breed of children who are totally whinge-free. They take life as it comes and never complain. As adults they can cope with all the major disasters such as earthquakes, bad hair cuts, wet Saturdays and tickets from the parking police. Then there are those children who whinge because it gets them what they want. We must stand by our guns and prevent paying off.

With a child who is a born whinger, anticipate, divert, ignore, occupy, put in another room, go outside, play music, use time out.

- Give maximum attention for no whinge and, when possible, withhold attention for whingeing.

- When addressed, recognise the child is speaking, even if you can't answer their question immediately.

- When you make an unwise decision, be quick to say, 'I got it wrong.' A quick turnaround removes the need to whinge.

- When you have got it right, don't let whingeing change the referee's decision.

- Label whingeing for what it is: 'That's whingeing. I don't answer whingeing.'

- Set some rules: 'If you are quiet for two minutes you may ask again properly.'

Zzz: sleep problems

A disciplined sleep routine is essential for all children and adults. Some children need much more sleep and others run happily on less. If a child settles late, yet is fresh and well rested in the morning, they may be designed for a later bedtime. Often the child with low sleep needs will have a late-to-bed, early-riser parent.

Video games and television in the bedroom seem to stir.

- Every night we should go through the same sequence of preparation at the same time.

- Don't accept procrastination in six- and seven-year-olds; get them horizontal and hope the eyes glaze and shut.

- Only allow slight modification of routine at weekends, as late nights and long sleep-ins disrupt the week-day pattern.

- A busy mind stops some children from settling at night. Help them unwind and establish a routine that prepares for bed.

- Stories seem to relax, particularly when a child is old enough to read to themselves.

■ A few five-year-olds still come to their parents' bed each night. If everyone is happy with this situation there is no need to act. You can accommodate the occasional visit by placing a mattress on your floor, but they must lie down low and not rise to a higher altitude.

Children soon get fed up sleeping with the parents in the same way we get fed up sleeping with them.

Index